Childhood

Childhood

Poems by
Emily R. Grosholz

Drawings by
Lucy Vines

Accents Publishing • Lexington, Kentucky • 2014

Text Copyright © 2014 by Emily R. Grosholz
Images Copyright © 2014 by Lucy Vines
All rights reserved

Printed in the United States of America

Accents Publishing
Editor: Katerina Stoykova-Klemer
Cover Image: Lucy Vines
Cover Design: Simeon Kondev

ISBN: 978-1-936628-27-8
First Edition

A fixed percentage from the sale of this book will go to an international organization that works to protect and encourage children worldwide, by providing food and water, medical attention, shelter from violence, and education.

accents publishing

Accents Publishing is an independent press for brilliant voices. For a catalog of current and upcoming titles, please visit us on the Web at
www.accents-publishing.com

Contents

Listening / 1
Thirty-six Weeks / 2
Adopting / 4
Accident and Essence / 7
Putting on the Ritz / 8
Snowdrop / 9
Twelfth Night / 10
Autumn Sonata / 11
Through the Darkness Be Thou Near Me / 13
The Discovery of Rain / 14
Finitude / 15
Pirates of the Caribbean (Disneyland) / 16
Eden / 17
The Shape of Desire / 19
The Discovery of Puddles / 20
Primary School / 21
First Piano Lesson / 22
The Beautiful Game / 23
Real Bullets / 27
The Discovery of Painting / 29
The Stars of Earth / 30
Letter from Châtel-Montagne / 31
To My Daughter / 32
Au Revoir / 34
But They Come Back Again / 35
Roses / 36

About the Author and Illustrator / 37

Acknowledgments / 39

Listening

Words in my ear, and someone still unseen
Not yet quite viable, but quietly
Astir inside my body;

Not yet quite named, and yet
I weave a birthplace for him out of words.

Part of the world persists
Distinct from what we say, but part will stay
Only if we keep talking: only speech
Can re-create the gardens of the world.

Not the rose itself,
But the School of Night assembled at its side
Arguing, praising, whom we now recall.

A rose can sow its seed
Alone, but poets need their auditors
And mothers need their language for a cradle.

My son still on his stalk
Rides between the silence of the flowers
And conversation offered by his parents,
Wise and foolish talk, to draw him out.

Thirty-six Weeks

Ringed like a tree or planet, I've begun
To feel encompassing,
And so must seem to my inhabitant
Who wakes and sleeps in me, and has his being,
Who'd like to go out walking after supper
Although he never leaves the dining room,
Timid, insouciant, dancing on the ceiling.

I'm his roof, his walls, his musty cellar
Lined with untapped bottles of blue wine.
His beach, his seashell combers
Tuned to the minor tides of my placenta,
Wound in the single chamber of my whorl.
His park, a veiny meadow
Plumped and watered for his ruminations,
A friendly climate, sun and rain combined
In one warm season underneath my heart.

Beyond my infinite dark sphere of flesh
And fluid, he can hear two voices talking:
His mother's alto and his father's tenor
Aligned in conversation.
Two distant voices, singing beyond the pillars
Of his archaic mediterranean,
Reminding him to dream
The emerald outness of a brave new world.

Sail, little craft, at your appointed hour,
Your head the prow, your lungs the sails
And engine, belly the sea-worthy hold,
And see me face to face:
No world, no palace, no Egyptian goddess
Starred over heaven's poles,
Only your pale, impatient, opened mother
Reaching to touch you after the long wait.

Only one of two, beside your father,
Speaking a language soon to be your own.
And strangely, brightly clouding out behind us,
At last you'll recognize
The greater earth you used to take me for,
Ocean of air and orbit of the skies.

Adopting

I. Before

Three days of waiting for the ultimate yes,
The rainbow uttered on a speechless sky.
Nothing distracts us from our wish for you
Suspended somewhere in your makeshift nest,
Real, inaccessible.

You must be waking on the painted sill
Of possibility, tracing the strange
Curve and stretch of sunlight on the wall,
Sensing a presence lost.
Only a small idea to us now,

You fill the thoughts of your abstracted family,
Willing to chase the stars to Bethlehem
And find you as you are:
All that we recognize and never fathom
In any child, and all that we imagine.

II. After

Snow stormed on your birthday,
Stormed on the day we drove
Down from the snowy mountains
To bring you home.

Night after night you wakened
At midnight, three, and seven,
Not fussing, but still hungry
For milk and me.

I fed you, and then rocked you
Beside the glinting mirror,
Running water in the bathroom
To make you sleep.

Outside the snow kept falling,
And silvered in the mirror;
I rocked you back and forth
And standing, slept.

Between our sleep and waking,
To the sound of water running,
Those nights we both endured
A second labor.

Out of the separate strangeness
We drifted slowly together,
Aching down and inward
To make one rhythm.

One smell, one long caress.
A womb of whirling snow,
And you and I together,
Safely delivered.

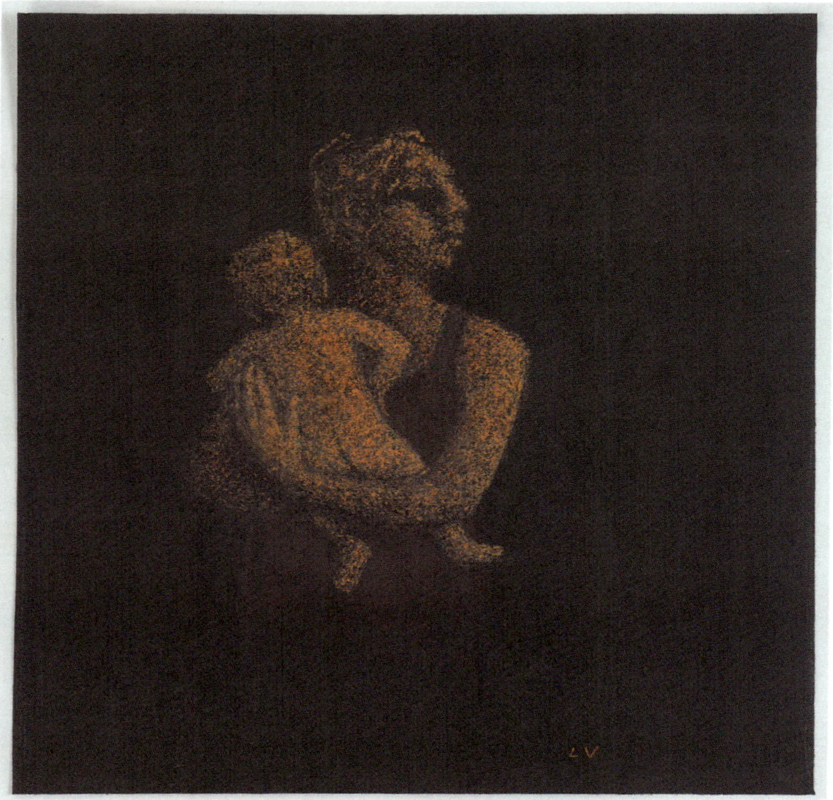
LV

Accident and Essence

Whose eyes are those? Bituminous black eyes
That shine with sheer inventiveness, and love,
And when they weep, burn with a smoky flame.
Dearer than my own,
They stem from people I have never seen.

All I can say of you began the morning
You were delivered whole into my arms
And suddenly we became
Mother and child, not interlocked by blood,
Only by love's half-accidental essence.

Your cry two flights away
Startles me up the stairs and out of sleep;
I find you in the dark unerringly.
All that I don't know travels in the light
Without allusion, like a daytime ghost.

Surely the nameless parents of your birth,
Their parents' parents and collateral kin,
Must often surface on your changing face.
But I can only guess them in your smile
That stirs and answers mine.

And so they gather, fleetingly refracted,
But real to both of us:
Your birth-grandmother's gesture when she shook
Her head in disbelief, and her tall husband's
Rounded cheek, his open-throated laughter.

Putting on the Ritz

After a long, cool winter,
At last in May a suite
Of warm days wakes the sleepers.

One covered from crown to root
In thick crepe skirtlets stops
Me, back from hibernation:

Loveliest of trees,
Big as the Ritz's balletic
Vases charged with bloom.

Not bought, not concocted,
Only improbably real.
Why am I not surprised?

My hair is snowed with silver,
Evidence how little room
Fifty springs allow.

And yet midwinter someone
Burst to life inside me,
And lately started dancing.

Just so improbably
Snow hung along the branches
Changed suddenly to flowers.

Snowdrop

Snow fell so early this year, just after Allhallows,
We never finished the ritual of raking clean
Livid grass and cushions of stricken moss.
The yard's still matted with leaves, oak, maple, walnut,
Visible once again as the snow recedes,
Tatted lace unraveling, going wherever the snows
Of yesteryear retire to, heaven or hellward.
Under the mat of crisscrossed mahogany
And black gold crusted with ice, one snowdrop thaws.

She stands already in the outmost bed, bordering
Woods, though it is only February, turned,
Dear smallest daughter, less than a week ago. I laid
The coverlet of leaves aside, and there she was,
Furled on herself and bowed, but blooming hard,
Sober, exquisite child of an uncertain season.

Twelfth Night

The Christmas tree is dry:
Resin-dropping twigs whose silky needles
Stroked my hand in Advent, break and crumble.
Time, high time, to take the strung lights down,
The ornaments that shiver,
And from the mantelpiece, the gilded star
Beside the homeless family it shone on.

Our house in space is here.
Our house in time is the terrestrial year,
Marked for us by the sun's near disappearance
In night and winter storm,
And those three painted fugitives, who huddle
Against the chill of a wind-riddled byre
To greet a mortal baby, small and warm.

Autumn Sonata

The ducks are raucous, flying overhead,
And all the talk you hear is running slower.
You don't quite get the words,

Not yet, but you can estimate the music.
Anger makes you weep, and a good laugh
Raises your toothless smile.

You stand to look, and listen as you sit
In the laps of people talking,
Wondering what the tides of life can carry.

Your hair is soft as milkweed;
Your father and I caress your head
Whenever we hold you, half unthinkingly,

And you move up against that stroking hand.
Your body curves along us when you're full
And arches when you're hungry.

We speak to you by name
And you look sideways, willing but mystified,
Trying hard to grasp at dancing straws,

To sing, to show, to answer, to remember
One by one the grape leaves as they tumble,
Somber oak and yellow jewelweed.

And yet for the most part you soon forget.
And yet I write this down
So you can tell us later what it means.

My voluble, mute son,
Who listen as the birds go storming south,
You know the melody, but not the words.

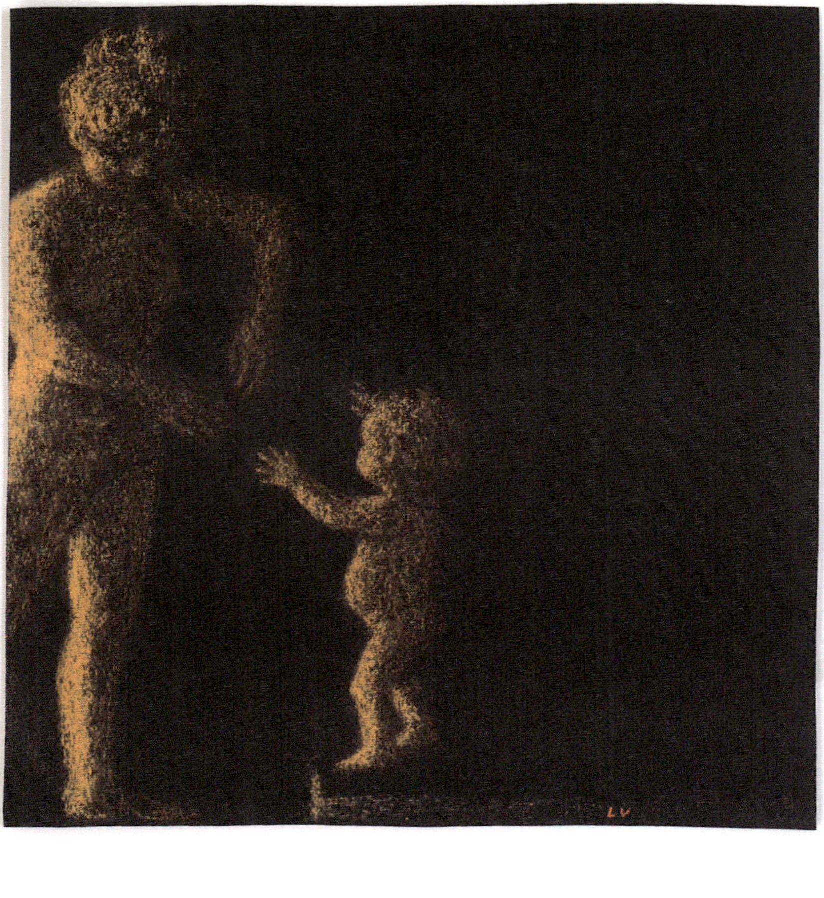
LV

Through the Darkness Be Thou Near Me

Sometimes I sit beside you in the dark
As you push off towards sleep,
Your bed a boat descending oceanward
Along the Serpentine.

Torn by other tasks (the house undone,
The word unwritten), still I like that waiting
When everything falls quiet, even you,
Even my restlessness.

The whirr from your cylindrical machine
Supposed to purify the air
Of pollen, mold, and dust,
Leaves silence nonetheless impure.

Hidden, the pilot light
Beside the dial bathes half your room
In vague, unsettling green,
The radiance of nightmare.

But lady earth respires
Against her million pillows, and the pea
Of fire. Trees scrub the local atmosphere
Till midnight's sweet again. And you,

Treeflower, porous leaf,
Breathe lightly, stirred as if a wind
Were lifting all the edges of your dream,
And fall asleep.

The Discovery of Rain

Barefoot, bare headed
Except for those luxuriant black curls,
The baby stands at play in April grass.

Rain starts suddenly, lightly,
So at first he notices
Not at all. Then touches

His curls, to find them damp and dampening.
Touches the earth, discovers
Something new that changes everything.

Looks up to know the source
And sees just leaves and air,
But goes on looking up because

—Reality or dream—
It pleases him to be
Watered by warm rain.

Finitude

Awake before dawn, my son and I sit drowsing,
Lapsed from a dream, louring toward consciousness,
Nursing a little, musing, counting our toes.
There are always ten, no matter where we begin.
Oh, look. He suddenly points at the closed door-windows
That cast over snow, past spindly lank silhouettes
Of maple, oak, black walnut, into the dawn.

On tiptoe, weaving, he runs up close to the windows
Charmed by the panels of gold set high among mullions
Of boles, the roses fastened in tracery-branches.
Yet how the fastening ravels: our matins are sung,
The windows beyond the windows wither away,
And then he returns to my arms asking his questions
In an ancient, unknown tongue. And all of my answers,
Equally enigmatic, are kisses in shadow.

Pirates of the Caribbean (Disneyland)

What begins as a slow drift into half-light
Suddenly accelerates: a plunge into darkness
Accompanied by rending voice-over screams
And then a world of cannon fire and carnage:
Bodies float up around us, dry land ignites.

All fake, but who's to tell you that, my smallest
Easily-startled baby? In my arms
At first you wince and shiver, then go rigid—
I'd save you, but we're prisoners of a moment
Explosively contrived for older children.

So, utterly unequal to the hoopla
And razzle all around us, you give up,
Turning to nurse. The pow of invented chaos
Withdraws behind the stillness of my body
That bends and opens just the same as always.

My body is your means of reckoning:
Three stars above, the gulf stream warm below,
My arms the coast your little craft stays close to.
Later, my love, when you set out alone
On deeper, colder waters, take my soul.

Let all the things we used to say return
Like angles among lighthouses and planets
For you to make your own triangulations,
And all we left unspoken, warmer currents
Threading the chilly maze of kelp and coral.

Material or not, my body's yearning
For the grown child it nourished once will stay:
Archipelagos scattered towards the horizon,
Involuntary tremors on the sail,
The great world rounded and a long way home.

Eden

In lurid cartoon colors, the big baby
Dinosaur steps backwards under the shadow
Of an approaching tyrannosaurus rex.
"His mommy going to fix it," you remark,
Serenely anxious, hoping for the best.

After the big explosion, after the lights
Go down inside the house and up the street,
We rush outdoors to find a squirrel stopped
In straws of half-gnawed cable. I explain,
Trying to fit the facts, "The squirrel is dead."

No, you explain it otherwise to me.
"He's sleeping. And his mommy going to come."
Later, when the squirrel has been removed,
"His mommy fix him," you assert, insisting
On the right to know what you believe.

The world is truly full of fabulous
Great and curious small inhabitants,
And you're the freshly minted, unashamed
Adam in this garden. You preside,
Appreciate, and judge our proper names.

Like God, I brought you here.
Like God, I seem to be omnipotent,
Mostly helpful, sometimes angry as hell.
I fix whatever minor faults arise
With band-aids, batteries, masking tape, and pills.

But I am powerless, as you must know,
To chase the serpent sliding in the grass,
Or the tall angel with the flaming sword
Who scares you when he rises suddenly
Behind the gates of sunset.

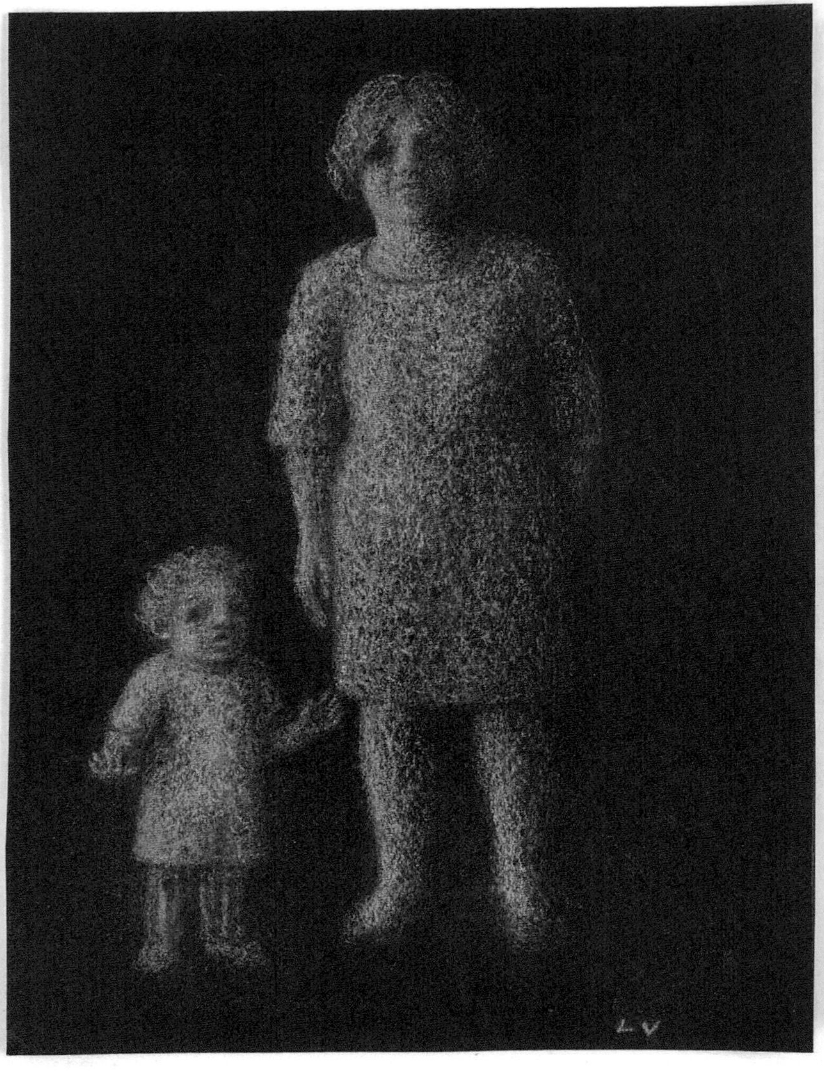
L V

The Shape of Desire

Tracing an airplane's pale trajectory,
You always point, and finish, "Airplane *gone.*"
Waking from dreams about your babysitter's
Dark-eyed, clever daughter, you conclude,
"Lulu *gone*," and hurry to the door's
Long windowpane to see her reappear
Freshly composed from memory and clouds.
Now you can say the shape of your desire.

Now you believe that each sidereal item
Carries a left-hand banner to describe
Through curl and dissipation how it was,
That every friend is summoned by a name,
Even in parting. You are wrong, and right
About the frail parabolas of love.

The Discovery of Puddles

Standing in his boots, in contemplation,
He watches sun spring off the patch of water,
Then leaps. Both he and I
Start at the burst and magnitude of spray,
Our sudden decoration of muddy droplets.

"Plash," he observes, correctly, and jumps again,
While overhead a bird
Sings out its two-tone as if in applause.
Acknowledging the call, he answers, "Bird."

His joy is like mid-February sun,
Snowdrops blooming early,
The irresistible, delicious cry
Plied by the bird above. I do not say,

"Stop it. You're getting dirty. What a mess."
My irritable mother-tongue is silenced
By the great flood of light,
Two words uttered truly by my child
Splashing in boots of diamond-spangled mud.

Primary School

My four children learned to read here, to talk back
And repent in the principal's office, to unlock
The ivory puzzle-box of the multiplication tables,
To utter a few lovely phrases of Japanese,
To marry and give birth and die in imaginary
Covered wagons laboring from St. Louis to Sacramento.

Today my daughter read an essay to the assembly,
And my youngest son played a Mozart air on his fiddle,
So for the last time I visited their first school, Easterly,
Namesake perhaps of the morning star, that shines
Only a little while before and after dawn, though secretly
It is also the evening star, and the errant planet Venus.

Fourteen years under this tangle of elm trees, lindens,
Black walnuts, pin oaks that rust bronze in October,
Maples that launch their bright wings downwards in April.
I wrote my name on a paper badge marked 'visitor,'
And kept it afterwards, as if it might somehow later
Reopen the doors, sealed now by the guardian of years.

First Piano Lesson

For years they have been pressing the white keys,
Sometimes the black, occasionally, haphazardly
Great fingerfuls together. But where
Exactly was the music, they wondered? Gone.

Today they built a bridge from C to G
As if across Giverny's garden pond.
Perhaps it is a rainbow? G to C,
Aural, slant-visible, inevitable, clear.

They stand amazed around the grand piano
Capable at last of lifting up
From sound's long restlessness the dripping
Glittery net of intervals and in its knotted strings

That golden fish, a song!

The Beautiful Game

I.

Forces unexpected, untoward sweep
Up and down the field at cheetah speed,
Wind speed, indeed sometimes the dervish turbine
Of victory-defeat seems to spin round
Faster than sound, or light, and therefore time.
Stars racing away from me, then racing home.

Lion rounding antelope, gazelle eluding
Sudden night beneath the leopard's paw
Printed with stars, that mortal circulation
Tracks the green pitch as if turf were veldt,
Kilimanjaro veiled in muslin snow
Where I stand by, all eyes, watching the clouds

Dousing the sunlight shining here and there
Against the players as they track the ball,
Feint, block, fill up the spaces on the field where
Offense and defense meld like sun and shadow.
How does the match turn out? I never know,
Win, lose or draw, the way my children dazzle.

II.

Along the edges of the soccer pitch
The maple trees are coming into focus.
Shoals of coral lace, or islands in the air
Whose gradients are differential flowers
Too fine to see against the upper branches.
My son commands the center of the field.
His boots are yellow and his shirt is silver.
We're down two-one, the sun sets in the corner

And turns the same light color as the trees.
Eleven on a side. I want my child
To win, but he is one soul among many,
And I am just his mother, sunstruck, silent,
Tracking shifts of wind, or luck, or mind
Beneath the drifting russet-argent. *Goal.*

III.

Driving my black-eyed son to a tournament
Where he'll show off his striking physical brilliance,
Moving the soccer ball as the wind shifts sand
To fashion a sinusoidal wave-edge over dunes,
I notice the emerald hills of Pennsylvania
Silent beneath a Sunday afternoon.
How smooth the hills are, polished, almost flawless.

But wait! Beneath that seamless green illusion
A thousand deer are moving, a myriad squirrels
Rake the earth for walnuts, the dim earth stirred
By a million earthworms frothing the under-matrix.
And mountain laurel blossoms burst into whiteness
And rhododendrons mauve, distraught by bees;
Ferns unfurl and violets fold their lanceolate leaves.

And all the oaks, wild apples, dogwoods, locusts
Breathe our excess, stale excrescence, deeply in
And out sweet rolling waves of air. O hills,
So like my hand posed briefly on the dashboard,
Beneath whose steep abysm a billion billion
Billion carbon atoms skitter under the flail
Across that bright invisible threshing floor.

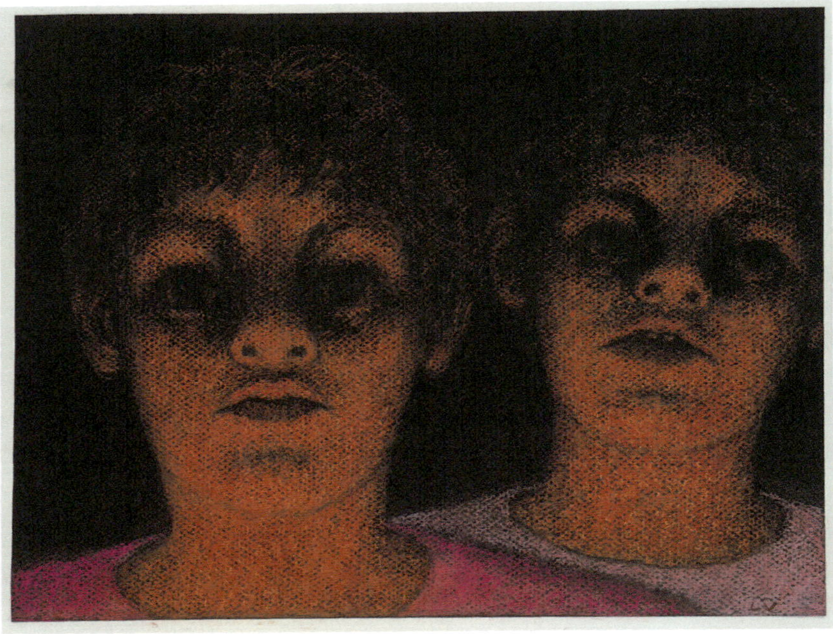

Real Bullets

My firstborn child, son of the right hand,
Goes everywhere lately fabulously armed
With silver F-4 bombers, Messerschmitts,
Empty .38's and plastic rifles
Loaded with spongy projectiles that still hurt.

His thirst for battle lore is a tin cup
Whose bottom drains the Marianas Trench
And salty gallons of enemy engagements,
Air corps daring over German cities,
Fleets of destroyers carving the Pacific,

Flow in every day at breakfast, lunch,
And dinner from his well-instructed father,
Child himself of a Navy career man
Who used to leave his children six months yearly
To sweep the minefields of a finished war.

"Why didn't Dad grow up and join the Navy
Like Grandpa?" My eldest son examines me,
Somehow embarrassed. "Son, in fact your father
Tried hard not to get drafted. He never wanted
To land in Viet Nam, sunk in a bad war."

"What's 'drafted'?" "Usually governments in wartime
Exercise their right to make citizens
Fight as soldiers. Male citizens," I add,
Turning to face my little boy, uncertain
Whether he understands. He understands.

"What?" he demands, suddenly agitated.
"You mean our government could *make* me fight?
You mean they could send me out on a battlefield
To get shot? Send me out in the open where enemy
Guns would really be shooting at me? Real bullets?"

The Messerschmitt nosedives to the kitchen floor,
And my small soldier, son of the right hand,
Is weeping, hard. And I, who equally suddenly
Understand the old doom of bearing sons,
Weep with him, and we fall in each other's arms.

The Discovery of Painting

Our studio is a cave behind a green door
Built into a hillside riveted by stairs
Like the improbable door I entered once
To see the ochre creatures of Altamira
Still breathless after thirty thousand years,
Flanks heaving from the chase, restrained, elusive.
How that low plastic ceiling pressed them down
On every speechless tourist, every random
Curvature of rock made flesh and bone
By some archaic brush, some vanished hand.

Now my son stands against his easel, speechless
Before the depths of red, black's utter midnight.
He dips and stabs: the paper's whiteness fizzles.
His mark's the birth of a new star, a nova
Blindingly there on nothing's facelessness
That also blinds. His mark is not a face,
More the proposal of his lust for pigment.
I think he wants to eat those ancient colors
Warping the paper, glutting the stubby brush
Suspended in his visible bright hand.

The Stars of Earth

Come away, come outside *now*, we whispered to the children
Who, that summer's night, were plastered to the noisy screen
Of their electric muses, cell phone, television, texting, Word.
They tumbled from their couches anyway, half-roused, and
    followed

Blindly across the street and up the hill beside the churches,
Far to the edge of cornfields, looking down the valley's darkness
And farther away the darkness of uneven glacial hills, moraine
Fashioned fifty thousand years ago, years when there was no
    summer.

Darkness everywhere, and three awed children shivering in the
    warmth,
And as we turned back home, we came to a tree on fire with
    fireflies,
A veteran oak encrusted from crown to root with tiny
    disturbances
That pulsed and blazed as if they sang of love, but sang in
    silence.

Letter from Châtel-Montagne

Along the road that leads beyond the village,
Behind the church, late afternoon sun warms
A great stone wall. Among the coral bells
Lit by its passage, tiny hummingbirds
No larger than the frequent fat black bees
Hover and shimmer, trying to drink their fill
Though they are never satisfied. How small
Their nests must be, woven inside the grass.

When we return, evening has cooled the stone
And closed the bells. The hummingbirds are gone.
My son observes, their wings beat thirty times
A second, but the miracle described
Must fail to conjure them, and the frail flowers
Avert their gaze. Silence is evensong.
It is too late to show you what I mean,
Writing only with words from Châtel-Montagne.

To My Daughter

You are so small that shallow water
Breaks above your shoulders, but you stand
Straight with your feet in the sand,
Frightened, delighted.

Your salt blood, blue-green
In rivulets beneath the skin,
Draws you away from me:
You were the ocean's daughter
Before you were ever mine.
I too, before you were born,
Escaped my mother.

Little one, though you and I
Hold ourselves hard against
The tide of that great river
Rounding continents,
We are fluid at our center.

One day you'll take the waves
In your arms like a lover
As I do now, for hours
Half in, half out
Of that seductive element.

O ride forever on your diviner parent,
Though I am long dissolved away,
Ride over the crests, as bright,
As fine, as wildly play.

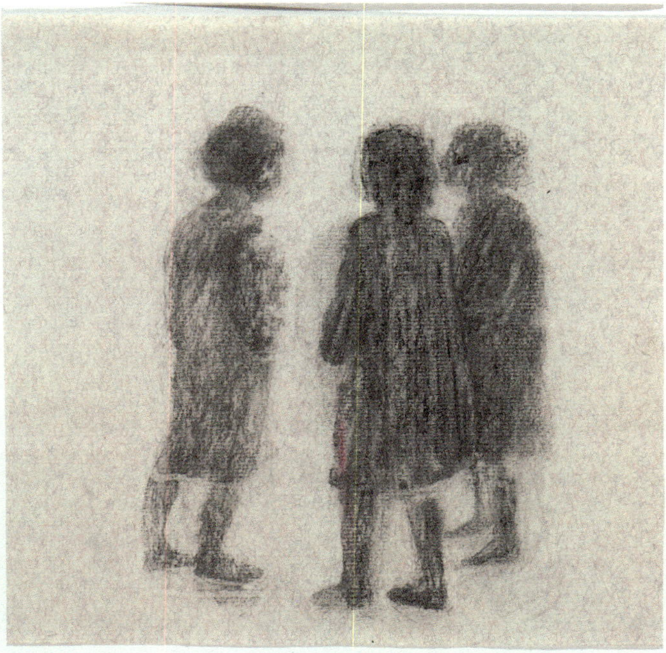

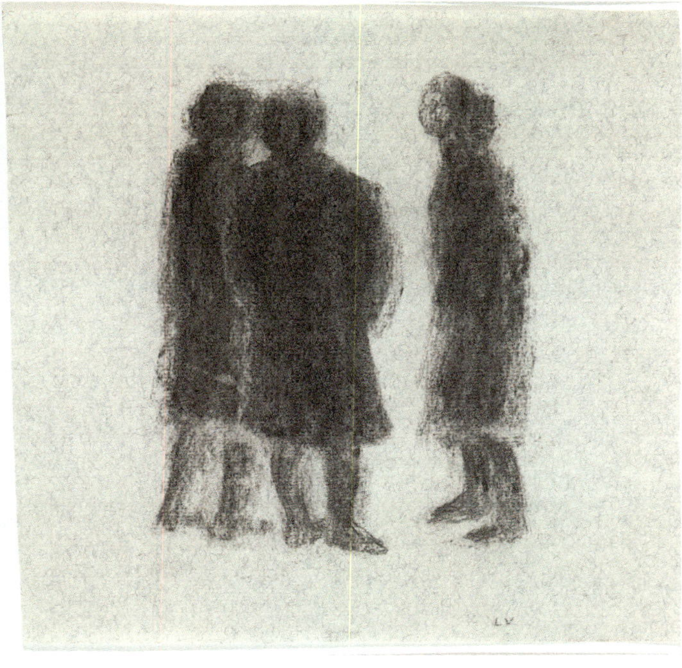
LV

Au Revoir

My girl sings in her room, alone,
One of the thousand songs she knows
By heart, uploaded sideways on her iPod
Molecule by molecule, soundlessly strung,
Effortlessly flung across innumerable
Times and infinitesimal blue spaces.

So sweet. Her true soprano warbles,
Wobbles, rights itself and then continues on.
Flocks spiraling. How quiet this old house
Will prove in later years, when love
Summons my girl and all the thrushes, starlings,
Finches, doves and waxwings will have flown.

But They Come Back Again

Over in the lower swathe of meadow
Hidden between cornfields and a row
Of wind-plied cherry trees,
The butterflies were thick a week ago.
Now only a soft luna moth or two
Lifts sideways on the breeze,

The colder breath of sunset. Slowly turning
Home I think I see a painted wing,
Which proves a sumac leaf.
Another bright illusion, holding on
Like traces of the children, orison
Or gold-framed photograph.

Roses

A glowing line, a rosy tautly-drawn
And now unraveling, feathering streamline crossed
The lucent early morning blue of sky
Beyond high windows, here in the château.

It was a sign, and wasn't. Another line
Bisected it, another slowly traced
A parallel of lanes: flight patterns over Paris.
Everyone wants to come to earth at dawn.

Great events involve men on the move
With guns and tanks, explosions in the air
Falling to ground as stars, then cloudy ash,
Then chemicals that kill thirty years later.

When I first came to Paris, walls were often
Scored with bullet holes, as a reminder.
Now the walls are plastered or filled in,
Or I forget to see what I remember.

Now that I'm getting old, I fail to see
Catastrophe as greatness. The bright lines
Lead to my rosebush on the windowsill,
Indoors not out, and lowly aerial.

The rosebush of the twentieth century,
Despite its charnel greatness, bore two flowers:
One vote, one soul and *school for every child*,
Honored often in absence, but still honored.

Praise the roses, tend the soil and water,
Vote twice yearly, raise your children well
So they can read the writing on the walls
And in the sky, before it fades and falls.

About the Author and Illustrator

Emily Grosholz grew up in the suburbs of Philadelphia, and has taught philosophy at the Pennsylvania State University for thirty-five years, with sojourns in France, England, Germany, the Netherlands, Israel, Finland, Costa Rica, Russia, Greece, Spain and Italy. She and her husband Robert R. Edwards (medievalist, rugbyman, and soccer coach) raised four children in State College, Pennsylvania, surrounded by small farms and green hills on one side and the town and university on the other. She is an advisory editor for *The Hudson Review*, and this is her seventh book of poetry.

Lucy Vines was born in 1929 in Hartford, Connecticut. She was raised in New York City, then came to France during the McCarthy era and has lived in Paris ever since, in a milieu of writers and painters. She is married and has one child. The Morat Foundation in Freiburg, Germany, the École des Beaux-Arts in Nîmes, France, and the Maison de l'Amérique Latine in Paris have held retrospective shows devoted to her work. Her works are untitled.

Acknowledgments

The images in this book were kindly contributed by Lucy Vines. They are not illustrations of the poems; rather, over a period of time, she and I agreed that there was sometimes a correspondence among some of these works created independently. These drawings were published in *Lucy Vines: Oeuvres sur papier* (William Blake & Co., 2007).

The poet acknowledges with love and gratitude the support of a bequest from Virginia McFarland for the publication of this book. She is grateful to her and her family for their support over the years. She would also like to thank the publisher Katerina Stoykova-Klemer for her business acumen and for her own poems, in two languages. Finally, she would like to thank Israel Charny for his wisdom and role as third grandfather over the years.

Some of these poems were previously published in the following magazines:

The Hudson Review: "Autumn Sonata," "Finitude," "Roses," "The Discovery of Painting"

Sewanee Review: "Letter from Châtel Montagne"

Centre Daily Times: "Twelfth Night"

Prairie Schooner: "The Discovery of Puddles," "Primary School," "Real Bullets,"

Poetry: "Thirty-six Weeks," "Pirates of the Caribbean"

Michigan Quarterly Review: "Accident and Essence," "Through the Darkness Be Thou Near Me"

New Virginia Review: "The Shape of Desire"

Sewanee Theological Review: "Listening"

Connecticut Review: "Adopting"

Watershed: "Snowdrop,"

Lilt: "The Discovery of Rain"

American Suzuki Journal: "First Piano Lesson"

Some of these poems have been published in the following anthologies:

Mortals and Immortals, ed. D. Lampe, Burchfield Penney Art Center, 2014; *Strange Attractors: Poems of Love and Mathematics,* eds. JoAnne Growney and Sarah Glaz, A. K. Peters, Ltd., 2008; *The Shape of Content: Creative Writing in Mathematics and Science,* eds. M. Senechal, C. Davis, J. Zwicky, A. K. Peters, Ltd., 2008; *Conversation Pieces: Poems that Talk to Other Poems,* ed. K. Brown, Knopf, Everyman's Library, 2007; *Mathematical Love Poems,* eds. JoAnne Growney and Sarah Glaz, A. K. Peters, Ltd., 2008; *The Shape of Content: Creative Writing on Mathematics and Science,* eds. M. Senechal, C. Davis, J. Zwicky, A. K. Peters, Ltd. and Banff Centre Press, 2008; *Lineas conectadas: neuva poesía de Estados Unidos / Connecting Lines: New Poetry from the United States,* ed. A. Lindner, a bilingual two-volume anthology where poems are presented in both English and Spanish, Sarabande Books, 2006; *Contemporary American Poetry,* eds. R. S. Gwynn and A. Lindner, Pearson/ Longman / Penguin, 2005; *An Introduction to Poetry* (8th, 9th, 10th edition) and *Literature: An Introduction to Fiction, Poetry,* and *Drama,* eds. X. J. Kennedy and D. Gioia, HarperCollins Publishers, 1993/94–2002; *Words Brushed by Music: The Best Poems from the First 25 Years of the Johns Hopkins Poetry Series,* ed. J. Irwin, Johns Hopkins University Press, 2004; *The Spirit of Pregnancy,* ed. B. Goldberg, Contemporary Books, 2000; *Rebel Angels: 25 Poets of the New Formalism,* eds. M. Jarman and D. Mason, Story Line Press, 1996; *A Formal Feeling Comes: Poems in Conspicuous Form by Contemporary Women,* ed. A. Finch, Story Line Press, 1993/4; *The Virago Book of Birth Poems,* ed. C. Otten, Virago Press, 1993.

CPSIA information can be obtained
at www.ICGtesting.com
Printed in the USA
LVIC04n0545071014
407571LV00001B/1